MOVIE MONSTERS

DANNY PEARSON

Badger Publishing Limited
Oldmedow Road,
Hardwick Industrial Estate,
King's Lynn PE30 4JJ
Telephone: 01438 791037

www.badgerlearning.co.uk

2 4 6 8 10 9 7 5 3 1

Movie Monsters ISBN 978-1-78147- 825-7

Publisher: Susan Ross
Senior Editor: Danny Pearson
Publishing Assistant: Claire Morgan
Designer: Fiona Grant
Series Consultant: Dee Reid

Photos: Cover image: Christian Aslund/Lonely Planet Images/Getty Images
Page 4: Snap Stills/REX
Page 5: Solent News/REX
Page 6: Everett Collection/REX
Page 7: Courtesy Everett Collection/REX
Page 8: Courtesy Everett Collection/REX
Page 9: NILS JORGENSEN/REX
Page 10: © Disney/Pixar/Photoshot
Page 11: © AF archive/Alamy
Page 12: Courtesy Everett Collection/REX
Page 13: Everett Collection/REX
Page 14: Courtesy Everett Collection/REX
Page 15: © Starstock/Photoshot
Page 16: Courtesy Everett Collection/REX
Page 17: Moviestore Collection/REX
Page 18: Courtesy Everett Collection/REX
Page 20: Courtesy Everett Collection/REX
Page 21: Weta Collectors
Page 22: © AF archive/Alamy
Page 23: Everett Collection/REX
Page 24: © AF archive/Alamy
Page 25: Ian Nicholson/PA Archive/Press Association Images
Page 26: © LFI/Photoshot
Page 27: c.Warner Br/Everett/REX
Page 28: Everett Collection/REX
Page 29: Snap Stills/REX
Page 30: Bloomberg/Getty Images

Attempts to contact all copyright holders have been made.
If any omitted would care to contact Badger Learning, we will be happy to make appropriate arrangements.

Contents

Vocabulary

atomic   special effects

dinosaur   vampire

make-up   werewolves

series   zombies

1. Monster Films

Lots of horror films are about monsters.

In old horror films the monsters were strange beasts, like sea monsters and giants.

In newer films the monsters are aliens, killer robots and zombies.

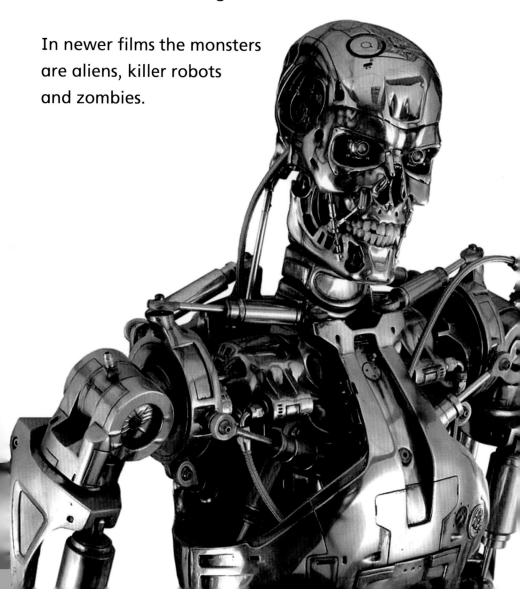

Old horror films don't seem so scary now.

But when they were made, people thought they were very scary.

The film *Robot Monster* was made in 1953 in black and white.

The actor who played the monster was dressed in a gorilla suit with a space helmet on.

Does it look scary to you?

MOON MONSTERS LAUNCH ATTACK AGAINST EARTH!

HOW CAN SCIENCE MEET THE MENACE of ASTRAL ASSASSINS? New SCIENCE-FICTION THRILLS!

3D

ADVENTURES INTO THE FUTURE in New TRU-3 DIMENSION!

ROBOT MONSTER

RELEASED THRU ASTOR PICTURES CORP.

with GEORGE NADER
CLAUDIA BARRETT
Produced by AL ZIMBALIST

In 1954, the film *Creature from the Black Lagoon* was made in black and white. It was one of the first 3D monster films.

The actor who played the monster wore a special wet suit.

Does this monster look scary to you?

WOW! facts

The actor could not sit down in the wet suit! He stayed in a pool at the studio to keep cool!

Even today, make-up artists spend hours turning actors into monsters.

In the film *The Lord of the Rings*, the make-up artists used 10,000 false noses and ears to make the Orcs and Goblins.

WOW! facts

During filming of *The Lord of the Rings*, an actor left her Elven ears in her car. When she got back, the ears had melted in the hot sun!

Of course, not all monsters are scary. In some films – like *Monsters Inc.* – the monsters are the good guys.

In the film *Despicable Me*, the minions were going to be scary monsters but in the end they made them cute, funny little monsters.

2. CLASSIC MONSTERS

There are some monsters that have had a lot of films made about them.

A vampire named Dracula has had the most films made about him.

Dracula is based on a character from a book written in 1897.

Vampires were said to be the living dead.

They would drink blood and only come out at night.

The first Dracula films were made in England by the Hammer Horror Studios.

More than 200 films
have been made about Dracula.

Werewolves are another classic monster.

A werewolf changes from a human to a wolf every time there is a full moon.

Actors used to spend hours in the make-up chair being covered in real animal hair.

In modern werewolf films the change from human to wolf is done using computer special effects.

This can make the monster more scary.

Frankenstein's monster is taken from a famous book called *Frankenstein*, which was written in 1818.

Lots of people think Frankenstein was the monster but Frankenstein was the doctor who made the monster.

Doctor Frankenstein stole dead body parts, put them together and made his monster come to life using lightning.

Some people used to believe that people could come back to life after they had died. They called these creatures zombies.

Zombies like to eat human flesh. Best of all, they like to eat human brains.

The first zombie film was *Night of the Living Dead*.

In this film the zombies walked very slowly.

Most zombie films now show zombies that run after their victims.

3. BIG MONSTERS

Some movie monsters are very big indeed!

One of the best known monsters is King Kong. He was a large gorilla that was trapped and brought to New York. Then he escaped and destroyed parts of the city.

The first King Kong film was made in 1933.

The giant gorilla that stars in the film was just a tiny model. The model was only 46 centimetres tall and it was covered in rabbit fur.

When people first saw the film they screamed and screamed. They had never seen anything so scary before.

In the most recent King Kong film an actor played the part of King Kong.

Then, after the filming, the studio used computers to make the actor into the giant gorilla.

The first Godzilla film was made in Japan in 1954.

The monster, Godzilla, lived at the bottom of the sea, until one day an atomic bomb woke him up.

Godzilla looked like a cross between a dragon and a dinosaur, and he destroyed cities just like King Kong.

Roars

King Kong's roar was a mix of a lion's roar and a tiger's roar. Then the recording was run backwards slowly.

Godzilla's roar was made by rubbing a leather glove on the strings of a double bass, and slowing the sound down.

Godzilla and King Kong starred in a film together in 1962.

4. THE MONSTER MAKERS

Ray Harryhausen was famous for his special effects.

He moved models one tiny move at a time and took pictures on film. Then, when the film was played, it looked like the monsters were moving.

One of his best-known films showed skeletons fighting with men.

The scene is four minutes long but it took Ray Harryhausen four months to make.

Steven Spielberg has made many films involving aliens and monsters.

In one of his first films, *Jaws*, he and his crew made a giant model of a killer shark.

Peter Jackson and his team made all the films in *The Lord of the Rings* and *The Hobbit* series.

He has also made a King Kong film – can you spot him on page 21?

In all of these films he has used the latest special effects as well as actors in make-up.

5. Monsters from Space

One of the most famous films about aliens coming from space is *The War of the Worlds*.

In the 1953 film, the aliens had three fingers on each hand.

They had only one eye, which was red, green and blue.

In the *Transformers* films, alien robots land on Earth.

They use Earth as a battleground to fight their wars.

The *Star Wars* films have a lot of alien robots and monsters.

In the first films, the monsters were models, puppets or actors.

In the latest films, more of the monsters were made using computer special effects.

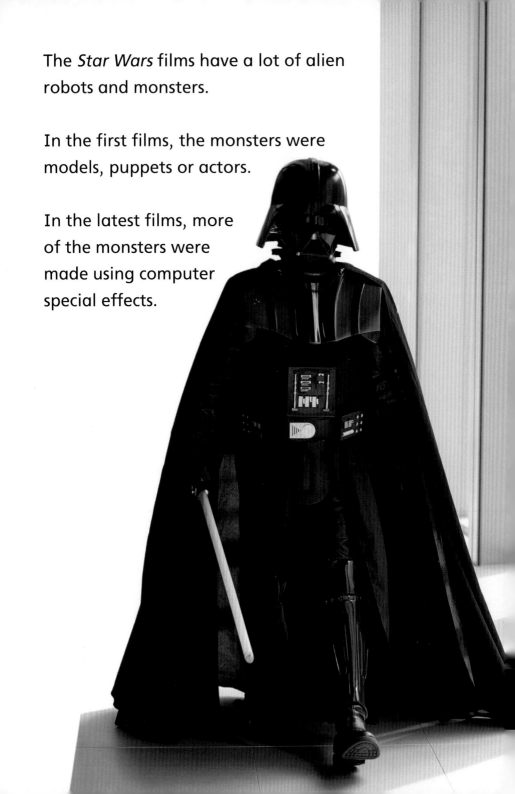

Questions

In what year was the film *Robot Monster* made? *(page 7)*

Name a film that has monsters in it that are not scary. *(pages 10 and 11)*

What are the monsters in the film *Despicable Me* called? *(page 11)*

Who was Frankenstein? *(page 16)*

What was the title of the first zombie film to be made? *(page 18)*

Where did Godzilla come from? *(page 22)*

INDEX